IMAGES OF ENGLAND

WORCESTER

IMAGES OF ENGLAND

WORCESTER

PAUL HARRISON

TEMPUS

Frontispiece: Friar Street, Worcester's most complete surviving medieval street, at sunset after autumn showers, October 2005.

First published 2005

Tempus Publishing Limited
The Mill, Brimscombe Port,
Stroud, Gloucestershire, GL5 2QG
www.tempus-publishing.com

British Library Cataloguing in Publication Data.
A catalogue record for this book is available from the British Library.

ISBN 0 7524 3726 7

Typesetting and origination by Tempus Publishing Limited.
Printed in Great Britain.

Contents

Acknowledgements

My thanks go to The History Centre at Worcester, and in particular to Robin Whittaker and Val Brown for access to their photograph resource and to the various staff there who put up with my irregular sessions.

I am also grateful to Mark Newton of Worcestershire County Cricket Club, Jenny Cheshire of Worcester Racecourse and Catherine Sloan of The Elgar Birthplace Museum for their time and for trusting me with their archives.

Many thanks also to, in particular, Adam Fradgley of the *Birmingham Post and Mail*, Alyson Rogers of English Heritage and Maggie Burns of Birmingham Library Services for their rapid turnaround of my very last-minute e-mails. And to all those, unnamed or forgotten, whose vision and enthusiam has left us with our photograph heritage.

Specific photograph credits appear in brackets after captions.

Introduction

Cities change. Successive planners influence layout and purpose; companies and individuals develop their buildings' appearance; and people come and go. Tastes, styles and trends change with the years and with collective interest, but inertia often dominates, and anachronisms litter the cityscape.

This eclectic mix, or mess, left at any one point in time does not, as film set designers would have us believe, give a snapshot of a period, but instead shows a complex mélange of architectural and stylistic evolution, as the parts of a city's sum grow and change in stubborn opposition to any order of its parts. Photographs taken over a period of years inevitably reveal a catalogue of such irregular development.

The photographs in this book are not, for all these reasons, a record of a particular time (you could accomplish this for yourself by walking around with a camera) but form a collection of what has been, but is no more; what is recognisable, but is unfamiliar. Each frame is the result of a design decision by the photographer, who may have been fully aware of this transience and felt the need to capture it for posterity (and here is that posterity in your hands), or may have wanted to create art. They are each, in their own way, intriguing, fascinating and sometimes, perhaps, a little tragic.

A History of Worcester

When the Romans came to Worcester in the first century AD, they built their settlement on an existing Iron Age site. The Roman town is likely to have included a road echoing the line of today's the High Street and northward, and their bridge across the river allowed not only control of the Severn, but a route to the troublesome Welsh. The shape of the current city of Worcester was further laid out by the 'salt road' built to Droitwich, following the route from the city centre up Lowesmoor and Rainbow Hill. Worcester's position would have made it a key distribution centre on a very busy river, with salt being sold to all centres accessible by water.

By the third century, Worcester had become a bustling industrial, agrarian and trading area, with its centre approximately where the cathedral is now, and iron smelting taking place in the area now bordered by Angel Street, The Butts and Broad Street. After this time, Worcester declined, possibly because the Diglis Basin was silting up and the river was becoming unusable as a harbour. By the seventh century, however, Worcester's fortunes had turned again, and it had a new role as a major centre for Christianity, with several established churches and a bishop overseeing areas as far away as what is now Gloucestershire and Warwickshire.

The population by the end of the tenth century was approximately 1,500 and at this time a monastic community first appeared, along with St Mary's Cathedral to house it. This early building remains as part of the crypt of the present cathedral. Although the town escaped the ferocious Viking raids further south, the Danish King Harthacnut attempted to collect tax from the city. The unfortunate collector encountered Worcester's sense of independence and outrage: the citizens murdered him and nailed his skin to the cathedral door.

By the end of the eleventh century, the city had spread up along the present the High Street through to Foregate Street, out to Cornmarket, and down to the river between what is now Copenhagen Street and The Butts. During the twelfth and thirteenth centuries, successive military attempts to control the strategic river crossing, particularly during the civil war between King Stephen and Matilda, caused damage to the city. The late medieval defensive city wall had five towers and fortified gates at the bridge and the castle, as well as several more recalled by current street names: Fore Gate, Trinity Gate, St Martin's Gate, Friar's Gate and Sidbury Gate. None of the towers survive, although part of the original walls can be seen in City Walls Road. The only surviving gate is the Water Gate that controlled access from the river to the cathedral.

During the fifteenth century, the city was engaged in cloth manufacture. The population was steadily rising, reaching 8,000 during the sixteenth century. The inhabitants lived in timber-framed houses built on the sites of older, larger, medieval stone houses.

The English Civil War took its toll on the city and Worcester's role in the battles is well documented. The first battle of the war took place at nearby Powick (1642) and the last in Worcester itself (1651). The 'Faithful City' was a Royalist stronghold until 1646 and was heavily defended. When Charles II arrived in 1651, his army was defeated in the Battle of Worcester and he escaped the city via St Martin's Gate, just east of what is now known as King Charles' House. The intense fighting, together with a long siege, destroyed the city's medieval suburbs. Rebuilding over the next century resulted in the predominantly Georgian appearance of the city's architecture.

Urban poverty was, by the eighteenth century, a major concern, and a large section of the city was living in squalor. In 1751, a group of entrepreneurs founded the Worcester Porcelain Works, partly to alleviate these problems. The combining of the firm with its rivals, and a royal warrant from King George III, who visited in 1788, led to the creation of the celebrated Royal Worcester pottery.

In the nineteenth century, Worcester's main employment was still within the clothing industry, by now specialising in gloves and protected, until 1826, by an import duty on foreign gloves. After this time, overseas trade started to erode the city's relatively expensive production and as profits fell, so, of course, did wages. The workforce and the unemployed were still mainly living in the medieval houses that had been divided and subdivided, the area between the High Street and the river typifying the urban deterioration into slum housing that survived until the sometimes brutal clearances of the twentieth century.

Worcester has always been a centre for transportation. At its peak, the Severn was the busiest trade route in the country and carried more traffic than any other river in Europe, apart from a small stretch in Holland. After its decline, the canal system both superseded it and revitalised it, as the locks at Diglis returned the river to its former levels. It was to be a brief period, however, as the age of steam brought the railway to Worcester, first to Shrub Hill and then to Foregate Street. In the twentieth century, railway transportation was itself overtaken by road traffic, and it is significant that the motorway age brought Worcester two junctions of the M5 within a few miles of the town centre.

Although Worcester has suffered from barrages of destruction in the past, either from military strategy or misguided municipal planning, it remains a visibly historic city, still with its medieval street layout apparent, and with many of its ancient buildings intact. Recent developments are being designed with more sympathy to the city's heritage and it continues to be an interesting and pleasant area to experience, either as one travelling through or as a resident. A walk around Worcester city centre can take the observant traveller back through Victorian, Georgian and Elizabethan times to the proud medieval streets still in evidence. Visitors to the magnificent cathedral or England's 'most beautiful cricket ground' can testify to the city's continuing attractiveness, and many are drawn to its events, including the Three Choirs Festival (hosted every third year here), the annual Worcester Festival and the Victorian Christmas Fair. With the music of Edward Elgar gently permeating the city, Worcester even has its own soundtrack.

Paul Harrison
September 2005

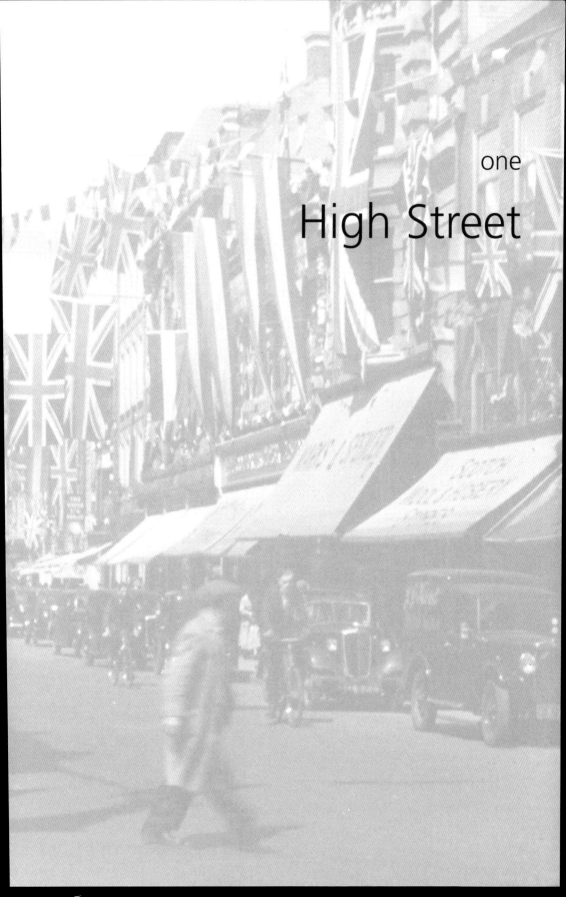

one

High Street

The area at the cathedral end of the High Street, approximately where the traffic roundabout is now, looking down towards The Cross. The road going off to the right is Lich Street, and is one remembered with some emotion by many. This is partly because it contained several historical buildings, including the medieval Lich Gate, and partly because of the dismal aesthetic quality of its replacement structures – The Lichgate (later Lychgate) shopping centre (now Cathedral Plaza) at one end, and a car park in Friar Street at the other.

Opposite above: Even in 1906, the High Street (literally, in Worcester's case, as the street is above the river) mingled the old and new. The large clock to the left in the photograph (still there, though the building has been replaced) is just in front of The Golden Lion, one of the city's many historical gathering places, and the last of the High Street inns to close down. The curved building on the corner of Pump Street was a more recent addition at the time (1881) and is now occupied by a jeweller. The building on the opposite corner of Pump Street, with the lower roofline, was replaced in 1925 and 1932 for Russell and Dorrell's furniture store (since relocated nearer the river). Everything to the right in the foreground of the photograph has now been replaced by a shopping centre. No light casual summer clothes here, despite the sun beating down on the protective window awnings!

Opposite below, left: The Golden Lion, patriotically decorated for some occasion, perhaps the 1953 coronation. Today the pub is no more, but fortunately some sensitive restoration has taken place, and the present coffee bar's interior has revealed a lot of original character in the roof areas and the front, though sadly the ground floor window is no more. Although the name has gone, the Golden Lion itself is still in place above the first-floor windows.

Opposite below, right: The same location in the late 1960s or early '70s, judging by the design of the signs on the two shoe shops either side. The Golden Lion sign above the first floor has been removed and replaced by something more synthetic, perhaps to keep the brewer's house-style, or maybe in line with the increasing trend of not raising the eyes above street level. Despite spotlights for the sign, a certain shabbiness is apparent. Nowadays, the building is still between two shoe shops.

A view of the east side of the road shows the Elgar Brothers' music shop in 1906. Sir Edward Elgar's father, William, and his uncle Henry operated from here, selling music, tuning pianos and organs, and providing an inspiration for the young Edward, who used to work there. These buildings, again, were victims to the shopping centre.

Perhaps the Elgars visited the Piano and Organ Saloon over the street at No. 101 (the High Street is numbered continuously towards the Cross, then back along the other side). W.W. Harris, dealer in images, has his own taken outside his shop.

Opposite: Another view of the south end of the High Street, this time in 1910. The presence of the printer and stationer is evidence of the activity of the book, magazine and pamphlet production that had been healthily running in this street since the eighteenth century. Another sign (by the lamp) proclaims 'Ye Olde Glove Shoppe Est'd 1798', which not only supports another famous Worcester product, but also proves that nostalgia is not just a recent phenomenon. The large building on the right is still there, currently a building society, but the premises next door went to create Deansway from what was then Palace Yard, outside the Bishops Palace. The curved-looking building in front of the cathedral lives on today, selling antiques. The buildings on the left of the street are all gone, and the carriage's rear wheels are at what is now the end of the High Street shopping centre.

The Guildhall uses its forecourt to good effect to accommodate the crowd which has gathered to hear the proclamation of George V as King of England in May 1910. National announcements of this nature have become the stuff of television, but more recent live events have not shown such a uniformity of dress as evidenced by this sea of hats.

Opposite above: This view is taken from Fish Street, looking at No. 13 High Street. The same view today still has the white painted shop on the right, though oddly the window next to the drainpipe has been bricked up. Number 13, however, is no more, instead you are faced with the monolithic glass front of one of the shopping centre outlets. (Copyright Mrs B. Collins)

Opposite below: The High Street (looking towards The Cross) is almost unrecognisable, with the shops mostly obscured by the mass show of patriotism for King George V's coronation. Having missed out on a coronation for the former king, Edward VIII, who reigned for only a year, the street display probably combined relief with hope for more royal stability. Perhaps the only recognisable name is Marks and Spencer, on the largest awning in the middle of the photograph.

Opposite below: During the early years of the nineteenth century, tramways came to the High Street, and here we have street improvements to accommodate them. The widening of the High Street near The Cross includes the demolition of buildings revealing an old timber-framed building that has been remodelled and re-faced in keeping with nineteenth-century style. All the visible buildings on the left of the street remain today, and at the time of the photograph, probably 1904, were recently finished. Broad Street leads off to the right of the photograph, and the clock just behind remains today, though in altered form.

Right: The High Street, during street widening for the tramway, *c.* 1902.

Numbers 3 and 3a at the cathedral end of the High Street, shortly before demolition in July 1963. The Embroidery Shop and Winston's carpet shop are having their final sales; in Winston's case the reason is made clear. (Crown copyright. NMR)

Opposite above, left: At the other end of the street, near where the High Street becomes The Cross, are Nos 47-52 High Street, looking like they are soon for the ball and hammer, probably in line with the alterations taking place for the new tramway at the turn of the century.

Opposite above, right: Later victims of demolition. Webb's furnishings shop relocated to Cornmarket when this store disappeared in 1935. Gertrude Mitchell Ltd next door (closer to the camera) survived for longer.

Gertrude Mitchell Ltd, whose minimalist clothing displays were attracting a lot of attention on this chilly but bright day. Despite the absence of traffic, Worcester had a pedestrian crossing here. Belisha beacons, with their distinctive striped poles and orange lit tops, were introduced in 1936, but the zebra stripes on the road that came to be associated with them did not appear until 1952.

Above and below: High Street shops were built on medieval foundations. When they were demolished in 1963, their cellars were photographed. This is evidence of the original building at No. 7 High Street, within the original city walls. (Crown Copyright NMR)

Worcester has always been a fortunate place for a traveller, with a tradition of good hotels and inns. It has also, during the last few centuries at least, offered a range of refreshment places for shoppers. Among others, the High Street has housed the White Tea Rooms and the Shakespeare Café as well as the Cadena Café, seen here in 1936. In those pre-war years, labour was more affordable and available, enabling the posting of a notice to become the craft of three people acrobatically managing two ladders, with a third available as a spare. (Copyright Mrs B. Collins)

Thornburn's Boot Market was located on the west side of the High Street and was a very successful chain store, having thirteen branches. The two white-aproned assistants are contributing to profits by offering customer service to a client each. The lady in the doorway already holds a neatly-wrapped shoebox and regards the man who is presumably her husband with a wary eye.

two

The Cross,
The Foregate and
Foregate Street

The Cross is the continuation of the High Street going north (away from the cathedral). In medieval times there was a cross and, presumably, a market. For cartographers, it has been the central point of Worcester. As commercial expansion continued, the main street flowed on beyond The Cross into The Foregate and Foregate Street, then The Tything. This view was taken at Easter 1928, and shows The Cross in full commercial flow, full, perhaps, of egg-shoppers. There is a steady traffic queue heading south towards the bottom of the photograph, either down to the High Street or about to turn off in the Malvern direction indicated on the road sign. The lack of public transport on the tram lines is perhaps partially responsible for the long lines of people perched on the pavement edges. The railway bridge in the distance indicates the location of Foregate Street station.

Opposite below: The Cross from the other direction, looking into the High Street. By 1902 the protruding corner buildings had gone and were being replaced by new structures in line with the rest of the junction, though remodelling continued for a year or two after. Broad Street (on the right) was then a major traffic thoroughfare, being the road from the centre that led directly to the bridge, and therefore all points west. The tramlines disappear round this corner and a carriage pulled by a white horse emerges. Most of the houses in The Cross have disguising awnings, but Turley and Co., together with The Worcester Mourning Warehouse have advertised themselves above these. The architectural mix in this street scene, though with an enforced coherence of style, creates a feeling of ordered individuality very much missing, and perhaps unattainable, in today's buildings. The quirky roof-level windows, not designed to be seen from the ground, only add to this.

An earlier time at The Cross, probably early 1900s, and people still linger on the pavement edge, though not the young man standing in the road more concerned with the spectacle of the camera than the oncoming cab behind him. The cyclist is turning into Broad Street on the left, though he too will have to dodge a man standing in the road preoccupied by some business of his own. A policeman lurks behind him, but seems more interested in the camera than any possible traffic accident. Dick's, the large shop on the left with the lights outside, was in the High Street, and was one of many shoe stores there.

The Foregate is home to Worcester's Hop Market, continuing today as a courtyard of shops. Barclays
Bank, along with a fine hotel, was built in 1904 and replaced the previous Hop Market. This photograph,
from the late to mid-1920s, displays the fine terracotta arches, bays and mouldings common to the whole
building. Despite the damp-looking ground, the sun is on the top of the building, and the chauffeur's
boots shine as much as the car. Barclays has since moved to the High Street, and a clothes shop now
occupies these premises.

Above: This view down Foregate Street towards The Tything was taken some time between 1881, when the tramlines were laid, and 1894, when the buildings on the right were replaced with the present library.

Right: A front view of Acacia House in Foregate Street, though set back from the road as seen in the previous photograph. This private residence is advertised 'To Be Let' in both photographs, though they were not taken at the same time, as can be seen from the difference in foliage. This photograph was most probably taken by the letting agents.

This is what the area looked like in 1925, when trolley buses had replaced the trams, and horse-drawn transport appears to be extinct. No cycles to be seen either.

Opposite above: Acacia House from the opposite direction, with its immediate neighbours, including Earl and Co., who are having a clearance sale. It must be near 1894, as Earl's signs read 'Must Sell – Premises Coming Down', together with 'Any Price Accepted To Clear'. No relocation for this firm. The house next door is presumably already empty. Although its shutters are open, all its curtains are drawn.

Opposite below: Acacia House, Earl and Co. and their neighbours were replaced by the Victoria Institute, housing a library, art gallery and art school. Opening in 1896, the foundation stone had been laid two years earlier by the future King George V. This photograph was taken in 1903, before 'rational dress' freed women from cycling in heavy, voluminous skirts. The house to the right of the Institute, with its distinctive iron balcony, remains, as does the Shire Hall to the left, whose railings can be seen. The Shire Hall was busy enough to have its own taxi rank, with a rest hut for the cabbies.

Looking towards The Cross, with St Nicholas' spire behind the tower of the Hop Market. The reason for the bunting is unclear, as this was photograph was taken sometime shortly after 1928. The glass canopy on the right belongs to The Star Hotel, dating from the sixteenth century and once Worcester's principal staging inn, with coaches departing every day for destinations all over the country. The first three buildings on the left of the photograph no longer exist, being demolished for the entrance to Foregate Street station.

Opposite, above and below: Two views of homes on the east side of Foregate Street that were demolished around 1931. They were two blocks away (south, towards The Cross) from the Victoria Institute. The Georgian façade echoed those of many other buildings in the street and retained an attractive visual flow without being regimented. Foregate Street was, at one time, regarded as one of the finest thoroughfares in Europe after its post-Civil War rebuilding. The buildings to the left of the Institute remain, but where this block, and that to the right of it, stood is now the home of Gala Bingo (formerly the Gaumont cinema).

These two photographs may well have been taken on the same day, as there is a 'Sunday' feel to them. They were taken in 1939 and show the Silver cinema from both sides: looking north with the shadow of the railway bridge over the building next door; and looking south towards the bridge. The Silver cinema and its neighbours are gone now, and the present Odeon occupies a very similar position.

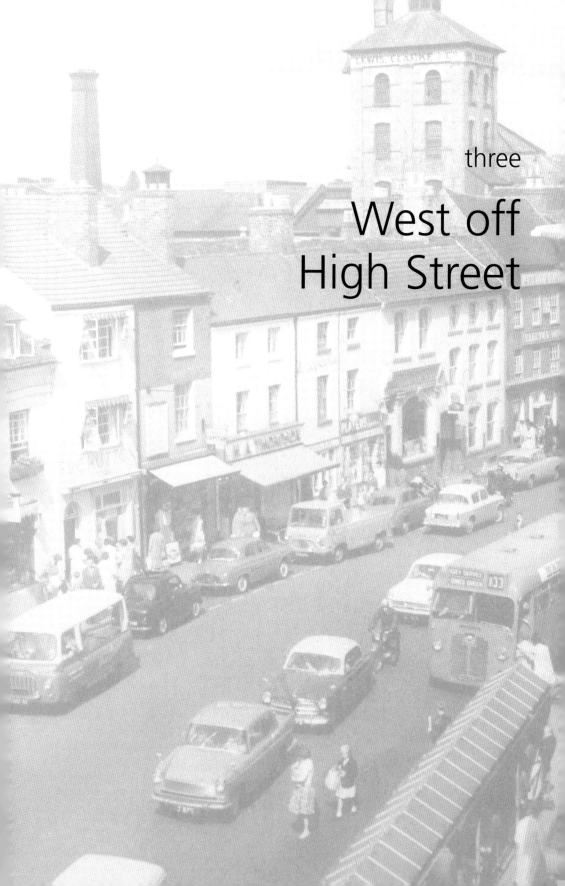

three

West off
High Street

Broad Street was once a very busy road, carrying Worcester's traffic directly to Bridge Street and then over the river. Consequently, it is the main road from The Cross and developed as a shopping street from early times. Like The Cross and the axis streets of the High Street and Foregate Street, it shares, in this photograph at least, the same elegance of individuality with shared Georgian style. Skan's tobacconist at No. 69 was a long-established firm who sold a general range of goods for gents and took pride in their window displays, though in the nineteenth century George Lewis had a very successful stationery business here during the boom years of letter writing. The current owners have preserved the building well, and the curved glass windows, now displaying Cornish pasties, are intact. Unfortunately, the next three buildings have disappeared since this 1950s photograph was taken.

Opposite above: One of these buildings, at No. 68 next door to Skan's, was this chemist, George and Welch, whose sign over the door gives away their famous secret identity: 'Late Lea and Perrins'. This was the shop where the renowned sauce was invented, developed and marketed before the two partners moved on to find fame and fortune with their new factory.

Opposite below: Lea and Perrins sauce factory looks today much as it looked around fifty years ago, when this photograph was taken. This is in Midland Road, near Shrub Hill station.

This is Broad Street, looking east. Not a very familiar scene now, as many of the buildings have gone, but there are two familiar names: Halford's cycle shop is the building that protrudes from the left-hand side of the street (in the far distance) – the vertical writing down the white wall spells out the name – and Marks and Spencer have a sign (just visible) on the third building on the left.

A view in the other direction, towards Bridge Street, and looking round the corner into Angel Place. A man is waiting for a bus further down Broad Street, but there are signs of roadwork going on, so perhaps his transport will be delayed. Charles Edwards, the wine merchants, has gone (the building is now a pub), with Edwards' sign replaced by a mural. The curved shop on the right in the photograph is also still there, though the street level façade has been compromised. The newspaper headlines at the bottom right of the image may date it: 'Crew Leaves As RAF Bomber Blows Up'.

Angel Place, which runs approximately parallel with The Cross. The building on the right is the same one as in the previous photograph, and some of the buildings on the opposite side of the road live on today. Most, however (from the raised roofline and everything to the right of it), have been replaced by the shopping centre that dominates the view today. Lewis, Clarke and Co.'s brewery and the chimney behind have also gone.

Passengers in Angel Place board a 'Free Lift Service' shoppers' bus. The poster on the left is advertising a film at the nearby Scala – Jane Fonda and Cliff Robertson in *Sunday in New York*, dating the photograph to 1963.

Angel Street, running from Angel Place to The Foregate, whose buildings can be seen at the end of the street. Dominating the view, and the principal building in the street, is the Theatre Royal. There had been a theatre here since the eighteenth century and in this view from the early part of the twentieth century it is in good Georgian shape, with a curved-glass canopy supported by decorative ironwork to protect its queues and those being delivered and collected by road from the elements. Because the glasswork overhung the narrow pavement, it was taken down in the 1940s, but by the time the theatre closed in the mid-1950s, another, simpler one had reappeared. Next door to the theatre, towards The Foregate, is The Shakespeare Hotel, a fortuitously named inn offering pre- and post-theatre refreshments. The other buildings offer a continuation of The Shakespeare's lines, and the street ends in a taller finale to match the structures on The Foregate. There is little remaining now: the inn is still there, now a cricket theme pub; the tobacconist shop survives without its shop windows; the theatre site holds a cuboid concrete Kwik Save building set back from the line of its neighbours, and the remainder of the buildings have been replaced by a modern brick block currently housing McDonald's.

Opposite above: At the end of Angel Place was a crossroads known as Fiveways because it met with The Butts, Infirmary Walk, Farrier Street and Shaw Street. The presence of a pub called The Five Ways is now the only reminder of this, since re-planning has split up the roads, and Infirmary Walk now ends further down. At the end of the nineteenth century, Angel Street carried round into this area, and Angel Place was a square, with Little Angel Street running a narrow path from it through to Broad Street. This is Angel Street Congregational church, formerly a chapel, now a nightclub.

Opposite middle: These buildings were on the corner of Fiveways. The photograph looks back along Angel Place towards Broad Street. The pillars are the Congregational church again.

Opposite below: The Scala theatre stood on the corner of Angel Place and Angel Street and at this time had become a film theatre. It is showing *The King and I* (1956) according to its posters. Next to it is the Corn Market. Both these buildings still exist, though the Scala is now split into a number of small shops.

Further up Copenhagen Street were these houses beside St Andrew's churchyard. The graveyard was through the railings on the left of the photograph and ran behind these buildings. At the end of the houses, towards the right of the photograph, a street runs off to the left. This was Birdport and continued across the street as Little Fish Street. This small thoroughfare was in about the same place that the much larger Deansway now cuts Copenhagen Street in two. All this is now gone, houses and churchyard becoming the gardens around the remaining spire.

Opposite above: The lettering on the Theatre Royal's canopy can be seen in more detail here as 'Denville's Popular Players', or the 'Famous Denville Players' depending on which poster you read, pose for photographs outside the theatre.

Opposite middle: While the destruction of Worcester's older architecture cannot often be excused, this photograph at least helps us to understand why it happened. These are the buildings between what was The Shakespeare Hotel and The Foregate. By the time this photograph was taken, in 1965, indifferent maintenance and inconsiderate shop-front replacement together with the removal of the entire second floor from several premises had left these buildings very sorry looking. Without conservation bodies lobbying for them, sharp, clean lines were to replace them entirely.

Opposite below: Copenhagen Street is nowadays a convenient but characterless route between the High Street and the river. At the bottom there is a pleasant square with fountains, but the street itself has a car park, a fire station and the rear entrance to the Guildhall. In 1928, this was the view looking up Copenhagen Street from the river. Like all the riverside areas, it had housing on both sides with a mixture of terraces and courts. As population increased, housing became overused and run down. These houses were occupied by artisans, particularly glove makers. St Andrew's Institute, at the bottom of the street, was a popular social centre. The church towers over the other buildings.

St Andrew's church, Copenhagen Street, sometime before its demolition in 1947. The spire, which dates from the mid-eighteenth century, was preserved and is known locally as 'The Glover's Needle' not only for its obviously pointed shape, but because the area around St Andrew's was the centre for Worcester's glove industry.

Three little girls play outside the Farrier's Arms in Fish Street, unconcerned about traffic or any other dangers of modern life. Perhaps a more innocent age, but an unlikely scene now, since Fish Street and its surrounds are no longer residential. This photograph was taken in 1960, before the housing clearances and the development of Deansway, quite close to this location, as a busy through traffic route.

four

East off
High Street

Left: If you cross The Foregate from Angel Street you will come to St Nicholas Street, which leads to the Cornmarket (now mainly a car park). This is a view from the Cornmarket, looking back to The Foregate, showing the Imperial Hotel.

Below: The Pack Horse Inn in St Nicholas Street is said to date from the fifteenth century, and was a coaching inn with more than ample stabling. Until the 1930s it was a Georgian-style building, but the nostalgia of the time restored or remodelled it into a neo-Tudor design. Today it is The Courtyard, a popular and very lively venue.

Above: The Pack Horse Inn can prove its heritage with this medieval-looking vaulted cellar, here being used as a cosy bar furnished almost entirely with barrels.

Below: The Co-op had quite a presence in St Nicholas Street at one time. This is one of their two stores about to be demolished in 1967. It is situated on the corner of Queen Street, the border road of the Cornmarket car park. The funeral director is still on the opposite corner, but traffic is now only allowed in the opposite direction.

The other Co-op store, dealing in fashions and drapery, on the same side of St Nicholas Street as the previous photograph, but further up towards Foregate Street. Fortunately this building survives. It was built in 1888, adapted in the 1960s with brightly lit window displays and a garish neon sign. Nowadays it is far more tastefully displayed and employed as a bar and night club.

Below: St Swithin's Street is off The Cross, opposite Broad Street, and leads, via Mealcheapen Street, to Cornmarket. There are some fine old low-rise buildings on the south side, backing on to St Swithin's church, and there used to be a cinema, The Arcade, towards the High Street end. It was formerly Central Arcade, containing shops. This photograph was taken before 1936 when the cinema was showing *Enchantment*, starring Mary Odette, and also, in a packed programme, *The Hope, Telemachus' Friend, Picturesque Britanny* and *Farmyard Follies*. Its plain and simple replacement building currently accommodates Superdrug.

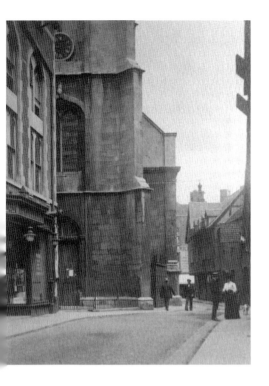

Above left: Church Street was once a pretty little street of shops, dominated by St Swithin's church, seen here almost straddling the street in this image from 1912. It runs from the High Street, meeting The Shambles at almost the same point as St Swithin's Street. Across The Shambles, the route continues with Mealcheapen Street. In front of the church, the little path to the left (with the railings) led to a very old well-established school. Nowadays, these old buildings house a restaurant. (Copyright Mrs B. Collins)

Above right: By 1938 the large shop at the end on the right-hand side of the street has had the black and white paint treatment so fashionable at the time. It is J. and F. Hall, an ironmonger and general store.

Right: This view of Church Street, from The Shambles up to the High Street, was captured on a wet February day in 1961. J. and F. Hall had diversified into such services as constructional engineering and domestic heating, and the City Arms has appeared next door.

Above: J. and F. Hall's building at
No. 1 The Shambles looking a little tired
in 1961. The presence of the 'Bargain
Sale' is perhaps a clue to its imminent
demise. (Copyright Mrs B. Collins)

Left: J. and F. Hall's building seen in
almost all its glory. Whitehall, not
Worcester, apparently, was to blame
for its demise, as plans to save it from
demolition were over-ruled by central
government. (Reproduced by permission
of English Heritage, NMR)

Above: In 1962 J. and F. Hall's premises were gone, and perhaps the only good thing to come out of it was this rare and temporary view of St Swithin's church. It would have been some compensation to retain this open vista, but instead it was replaced by a structure that was considered very unsympathetic to its surroundings.

Below: Continuing down either Church Street or St Swithin's Street, across The Shambles, the road is now Mealcheapen Street. This is a view back up the street looking to St Swithin's church. The sign for The Reindeer public house can be seen on the left, but the pub opposite it in the photograph is no longer there. The one on the right in the foreground is The Royal Exchange (now The Exchange) on the corner of Cornmarket.

E.M. Parsons looks like it has finished its sale and closed, the sign over the shop front having disappeared and the premises looking very empty. This is Mealcheapen Street going off to the right, with the photographer's back to St Swithin's. Trinity Street is in the other direction. The ladies at the barrow seem to be doing a good trade in this mid-1930s shot, and there may well have been a flower seller in front of the church.

The courtyard of the Reindeer Inn, from around the 1920s. The sun is filtering through the glass roof and a precariously placed baby is being juddered over the cobbles as flowers are being delivered. The Reindeer Inn was one of Worcester's old staging inns, and this would have been the way through to the stable block.

Years later, regular deliveries to what has become a pub are still being made, judging by the grooves in the paint on the wall. The roof has been raised above the little balconies and there is an airy semi-outdoors drinking area, though this was sometimes abused, if the sign that reads 'Fish and Chips Not Allowed' is anything to go by. Today the pub has gone, but Reindeer Court remains as a successful conversion of the old buildings into a shopping court with cafés and a restaurant.

Pump Street, seen here in January 1965, leaves the High Street opposite Copenhagen Street, and runs down to New Street. Now a pedestrian precinct, it has a few old buildings and some rather unattractive new ones. The interesting parts of this photograph are the gabled timber-framed shops at the centre, one of which has been rendered and painted. At one time this double-fronted building was the Horse and Jockey Inn, whose records date back to 1766, although it was possibly much older.

Left: The view from the other side of Pump Street in June of the same year. On the extreme left in the photograph is the Eagle Vaults bar at the start of Friar Street – the Horse and Jockey's former next-door neighbour. Further up towards the High Street was The Swan, housed in a similar timber-framed building. The Famous Army Stores has optimistically taken a short lease on the nearest half of the former Horse and Jockey, and 'will open shortly'.

Below: Number 29 Pump Street in October 1965, where the extent of visual and structural decay can be seen. Number 29 had gone through several changes of identity just prior to this photograph and displays advertisements for patterns, seeds, meat-rationing coupons, a temporary office for a Sheffield firm, teas and accommodation for cyclists, as well as the estate agents handling the premises.

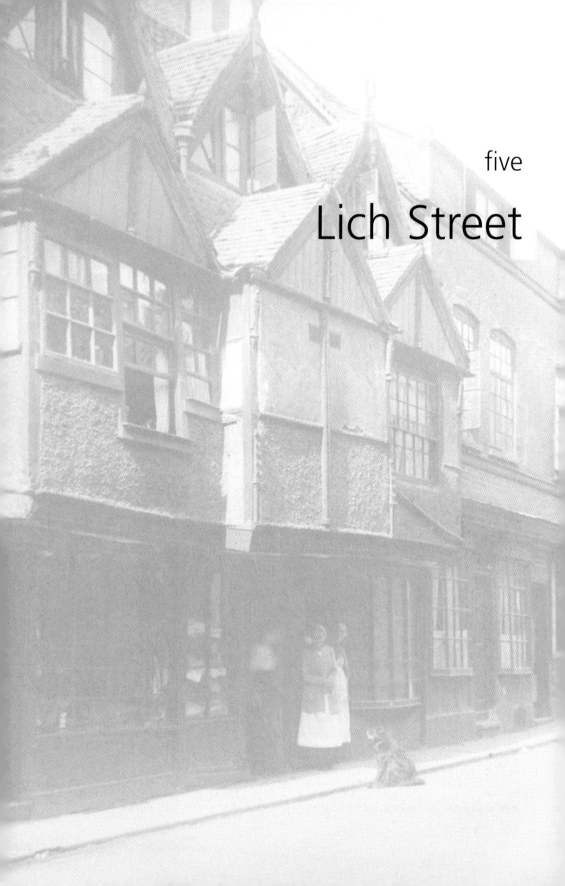

five

Lich Street

Lich Street no longer exists in any form. It ran east from the High Street, and, in 1955, if you had walked down the hill you would have had this view towards Friar Street at the bottom. Lich Street is named after the Lich Gate, which is the opening that can be seen centre right. This view is from nearly halfway down the street.

This is a view from the Lich Gate, looking at the black and white house, No. 23, seen in the previous photograph. It is only three years later, so little has changed.

Opposite above, left: This is the view from further down the hill. The black and white house can just be seen jutting out next door to A.A. Abbott's chimney-sweeping sign, and opposite is the Lich Gate. Dominating the scene is this magnificent four-storey building, probably an inn as there is a sign over the front window. Even by 1906, the buildings are looking shabby, and the pavement does not look like it makes for easy walking, especially late at night with little sign of street lighting.

Opposite above, right: In 1898, when this photograph was taken, the houses on the far right were condemned. The double-fronted house in the foreground was known as the Old Deanery.

Opposite below, left: The Old Deanery in Lich Street around 1925 – complete with ladies and a dog – looking re-faced and still holding up well.

Opposite below, right: By 1938, however, the building is looking very sorry for itself, with plaster broken away down to the wattle and the roof crumbling. It was let as cheap lodgings, and obviously had not been treated well by either tenants or landlord.

A lich-gate (or lych-gate) is a roofed gateway to a churchyard, in this case St Michael's church, and is traditionally used during a burial to shelter the coffin as the vicar approaches. The word 'lich' originally comes from the Old English *lic* and translates as 'corpse'. This was one of the last surviving lich-gates in the country, and a very good example that could have been preserved, moved or at least kept for a museum. In 1912, the year this photograph was taken, it was in regular use as a passageway between Lich Street and College Street. Although no longer directly leading to a churchyard, the church itself was through the arch and to the right, the Punch Bowl Inn was to the left.

By 1956 the Lich Gate found itself in this sorry state. Patched up and closed down, the surrounding shops are crumbling, although the gate itself seems ready to go on. Sadly, it did not.

Above: A sunny day in 1938, and Lich Street looks like a shantytown. The fine old inn from 1906 has had its upper floor removed and stands headless out of line; patch-plastering is reinforcing the walls and the buildings seem to lean together drunkenly.

Right: In 1938 this clearance area was recorded. From left to right, they are: No. 10; No. 8, a shop; the Lich Gate; the rear of No. 6 College Street; the rear of St Michael's church; No. 6 and No. 4. All were demolished between 1948 and 1956.

Many Worcester buildings were designed to be narrow and very long. Originally this was so that a business could be run from the front, and ample storage and living space could exist behind. When the population increased dramatically, these long houses were split up, but, because they were terraced, access was limited and they became back-to-back houses. The longer houses were split into several parts, often only with access from a central court or alleyway. This is the rear of one of these courts in Lich Street. The narrow entrance would run through to the front of the building, with doorways along it. Most of these courts became health hazards in the years leading up to the clearances in the 1950s and '60s, and so were demolished. However, some survive around the town centre, and are surprising finds from time to time.

In preparation for the Lychgate Centre the whole of Lich Street was cleared, and around 1966 this well was discovered and recorded. It had possibly been the only source of water for the house, or maybe the immediate area, for hundreds of years. Whether the subjects of the photograph are builders, archaeologists or photographers is not recorded.

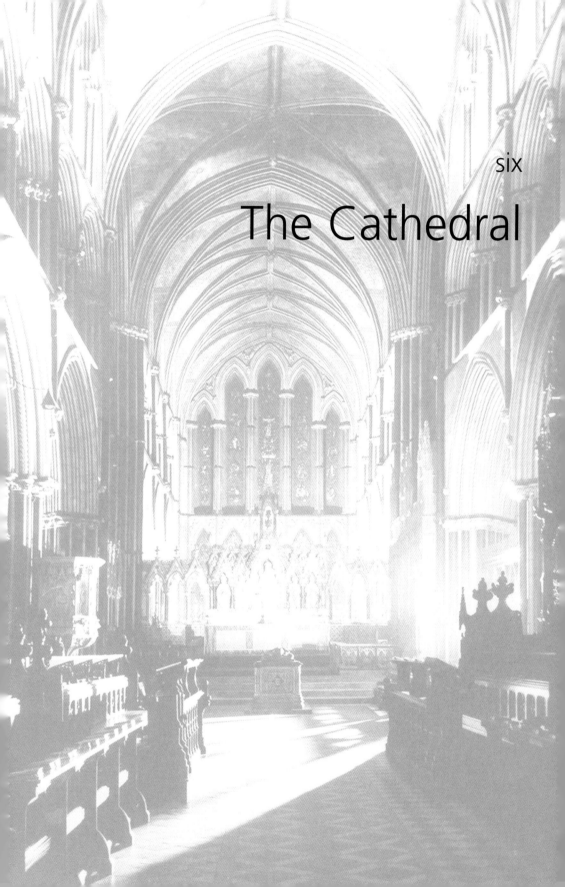

six

The Cathedral

Above: Worcester Cathedral seen from the location of the Lich Gate, *c.* 1960. With the demolition of St Michael's church the cathedral can be seen almost in its entirety. The road between the temporary car park in the middle and the cathedral is College Street, which then extended further. The area was awaiting development into the traffic roundabout by the shopping centre.

Below: The cathedral is, of course, Worcester's defining visual feature. The city exists in its present form because of the cathedral and it has always exerted a visual pull to those with artistic tendencies. Its location next to the river has preserved its open views and gives the impression, even today, of a more rural location. This scene was recorded on Easter Monday in 1952. (Copyright *Sunday Mercury*)

Above and below: Two views of the cathedral choir, showing both ends. The photographs give some impression of the space and scale of the building, which was extensively restored in 1854 by George Gilbert Scott, who also used his sense of Victorian grandeur later when designing St Pancras station, Midland Grand Hotel and the Albert Memorial.

Left: Excellent examples of medieval and Victorian carved stonework can be seen throughout the cathedral. Elaborate tombs abound, including those of King John – of Magna Carta fame – and Prince Arthur, elder brother of Henry VIII.

Below: The cloisters, seen here in a photograph from the early 1900s, offer a peaceful area to stroll, pass through to the grounds, or take coffee (slightly less peaceful when they house exhibitions).

Above: Below the cathedral is the original eleventh-century crypt, nowadays more effectively lit than in this photograph. It is the largest example of a Norman crypt in England.

Below: In College Green, on the south side of the cathedral, is the remainder of the medieval Guesten Hall. In former rebuilding of the cathedral, the hall was condemned as unsafe and demolished, except for one wall. Today, over 100 years later, the wall still stands, though bereft of its ivy and, sadly, much of its window tracery. There is even a sign in place warning of potential falling masonry. The other part of the hall that was saved was its magnificent timber roof, built in the 1330s, and now remounted in the Avoncroft Museum of Historic Buildings near Bromsgrove.

Above: Further round the cathedral are the ruins of its previous incarnation, the monastery. This early photograph shows the Water Gate, the only surviving medieval city gate. On the lower part of this, leading from the river, the various flood levels from over the years are recorded. The top three (in descending order) were 1770, 1947 and 1672, with little to separate them. The most recently recorded is November 2000. St Andrew's church tower can be seen in the background, in those days attached to a church, competing with the now extinct factory chimneys.

Left: Two boys gaze at the impressionistic reflection of the cathedral in the Severn while hoping for a catch. In 1905 the area was hiding behind a thicker tree and ivy growth.

A long-established ferry service took passengers the short distance across the river until it was closed, shortly after the Second World War. It ran to and from the Water Gate, seen here on the right in the photograph, with its steps leading to the water. The ferry service has returned in recent years, operating in the summer months as a money-raising charity enterprise.

Previous page: The chapter house dates back to the eleventh century and is a circular building with an impressive vaulted ceiling. It is now open to the public on various special occasions. The details of the two dignitaries are not recorded, though their presence here suggests that they were essential to the running of the cathedral in 1899. (Copyright Birmingham Library Services)

seven

Roads South

Left: The centre of this photograph, showing St Michael's church in 1954, is now occupied by Cathedral Plaza and the roundabout in front of it. The view was taken from the cathedral tower and the road in the foreground is College Street. The street behind it is Lich Street, and New Street and Friar Street can just be discerned running from top left past the half-timbered buildings.

Below: By contrast, this view has hardly changed in over fifty years. College Yard is the curved road that runs from College Street (by the roundabout) round to the cathedral door. Taken in the summer of 1953, the bunting is probably for the coronation. Fairly minor changes include the change of shop ownership (now Bygones of Worcester's antiques); the lack of ivy on the buildings; and the appearance of several iron posts on the pavement.

Above: The intricate construction of ropes, poles and pulleys around the South Africa war memorial, in the cathedral grounds, would not look inappropriate in a circus. It was there to facilitate a dramatic unveiling to the gathered crowd of the monument to victims of the 1899-1902 Boer War. The cathedral was to lose all its iron railings to another war forty years later.

Below: In 1918 the cathedral grounds were still the most public gathering space. Here, in March of that year, the Women's Land Army are campaigning under what looks like a biplane wing. How it got there is not revealed. With seven or eight months of the war still to go, the navy may well have benefited from their snappy 'Grow More Wheat To Help The Fleet' message.

Edgar Street runs off College Street. The Edgar Tower used to be known as St Mary's Gate, and was the main gateway into the cathedral and the monastic area, now occupied by King's School. College Green can be glimpsed through the gate. Although built a few hundred years later, it bore a statue of the eleventh-century King Edgar. In the early years of the twentieth century, the tower was restored, and this is a view dating from after 1912, when the statues were replaced. The tower's massive wooden gates are original, constructed on the orders of King John after the great Worcester fire of 1202.

College Street is the main road south from the cathedral end of the High Street. In 1899, this was the view opposite the cathedral across College Street. It shows St Michael's church with a violin maker's next door, and next to that the Lich Gate leading to Lich Street. To the right of this is the Punch Bowl Inn, which displays its name on the glass bowl of its ornate gas lamp and boasts not only locally produced ales on its sign, but also good accommodation for cyclists touring the area. (Copyright Birmingham Library Services)

The Punch Bowl was obviously a meeting venue for at least one company of like-minded people. These twenty-one men in hats are not identified, either by name or group, and the date of the photograph is not known, but the Punch Bowl seems to be unchanged in appearance from the previous photograph. The rather artistic appearance of some of the group perhaps suggests that they are painters, writers or musicians, or maybe even itinerant theatre people staying in the accommodation.

Taken shortly before 1966, this view shows College Street before redevelopment to widen the road. In the foreground is the edge of the cathedral grounds, advertising a performance of Handel's *Messiah*. Opposite, alternative entertainment is offered on a poster advertising Smart's Circus on the empty Cathedral China Shop. The entrance to the Talbot Hotel, via its courtyard, can just be seen opposite Porter's shop.

Above: Another view of College Street. Taken a few years earlier, in 1961, and viewed from the other side of the road, the Talbot's courtyard entrance is easier to spot. The entrance to Edgar Street is on the right, after the large building in the middle, and the 'No Left Turn' sign refers to Friar Street.

Left: Ye Old Talbot Inn looks inviting as it glows brightly in the winter snow of 1951. The inn has an interesting history dating back to the thirteenth century when it started life as the church house to St Michael's, and was accessed by a path through the churchyard. When the road was widened in 1966, the courtyard was much reduced and The Talbot was extensively remodelled. It now openly straddles the corner of College Street and Friar Street.

Above: Sidbury (meaning 'south of the borough')
is the southerly continuation of College Street,
after the junction with the City Walls Road. In
1898, coming into the city from the south, Sidbury
curved round to the right to become Friar Street,
with College Street on a left fork just before.
A weary traveller could find refreshment in the café
on the left or the Red Lion Inn opposite (now a
Thai restaurant). The focal point is the cathedral,
but the timber-framed building just before the road
that bends to the right is The Commandery. All
buildings visible on the left side of the road, up to
the junction with Edgar Street, are now gone.

Right: A little closer, and just two years later.
Sidbury's regular traffic is evidenced by the horse
emissions in the road. The Commandery, then
used as shops, is on the right (it lost the side
window during renovations later in the twentieth
century). The quality and care that went into
Victorian street lighting, as displayed in the
beautiful gas lamp on the left, is impressive when
viewed from our more utilitarian age.

In September 1957 the scene is rather different. The orderly line of shops leading up to The Commandery has been altered and painted in various colours; the street lamp has evolved into something brighter, but duller. The buildings on the left have been demolished for alterations to the canal bridge.

A little later, this old house was to go too. It stood on the corner of St Peter's Street, a short picturesque road of timber-framed houses leading to its eponymous church. All was swept away in the enthusiasm for modernism.

The view from the other side of the road in 1955 shows shops in the process of being removed from the south side of the canal bridge. The area is now a car park. The Commandery juts out on the left looking a little the worse for wear. It has also since lost the side window on this side.

As the clearance continued, this area was next. Bladder's motorcycle shop was a long-established firm, previously selling bicycles. On the opposite side of the street, the buildings in the foreground mostly remain, with the tall, gable-ended house now the end of the road, as the rest were demolished to make room for the City Walls Road. The low, twin-gabled café is now Charlie's restaurant and café.

Although by 1910 Bladder's had diversified into cars, becoming a cycle and motor works, their main business was still pedal-power. This publicity photograph shows how comprehensively stocked the shop was, being agents for Humber, Swift and Raleigh. Their support for the Cyclists' Touring Club is shown on the plaque above the window.

The change in use of the canal, from industrial to recreational, has benefited from the reconstruction of the Sidbury bridge. Previously hidden from public view, the canal and the lock on the far side of the bridge are now pleasantly exposed. Work had started, as seen here in April 1957, with the advertising billboards being taken down. All the houses and shops visible exist today.

In 1910, the bridge had undergone a previous rebuild, in which deep earthworks had uncovered the bastion of the medieval Sidbury Gate – the entrance to the city from the south. Either the antiquities or the presence of the camera has attracted a cross-section of the public to the viewing area.

Later in 1957, the bridge extension is in place for the road widening, though the wall has not yet moved. The present wall incorporates a plaque commemorating Sidbury Gate, which was stormed by Parliamentary troops during the English Civil War. The last battle of this war took place in Worcester on 3 November 1651.

A local artist sells his wares in Sidbury. The date is unknown, but the presence of the War Savings Centre dates it probably to the 1920s. The War Savings scheme, or war bonds, was so successful during the First World War that it continued afterwards and, of course, boomed during the 1940s.

Above left: Sidbury, like many other parts of Worcester's inner city, had its courtyard housing, and this was the view down No. 2 Court showing a rather dilapidated area, though obviously still heavily populated judging by the footprints in the snow. It was demolished at the end of the 1960s. (Copyright Mrs B. Collins)

Above right: Number 9 Court, seen from the rear in 1950. It was near the top of Sidbury opposite the cathedral, whose tower pinnacles can just be seen over the rooftops on the left.

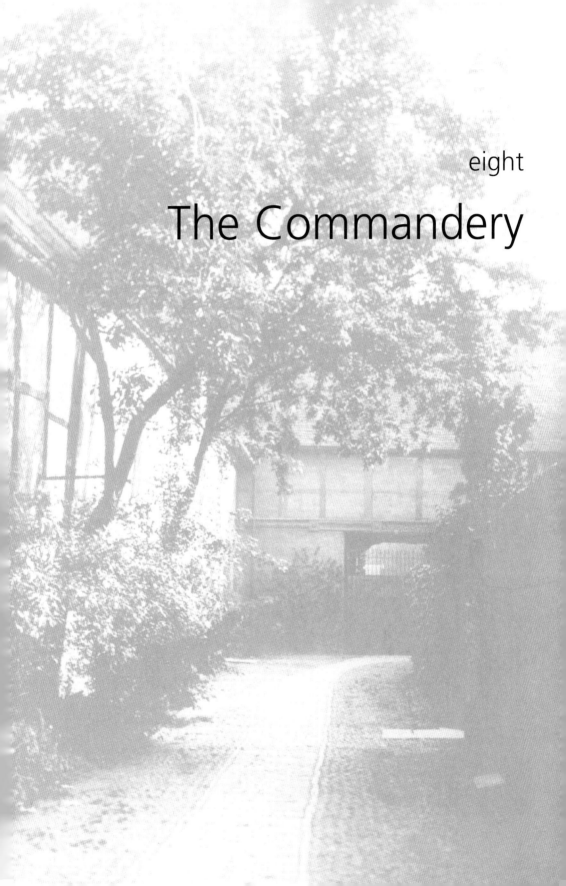

eight

The Commandery

A close-up of The Commandery frontage, as was seen obliquely in previous photographs. The main parts of the building, in an H-shaped formation, are behind, and have undergone many changes since it was created in the fifteenth century as St Wulstan's Hospital, attached to a church. At the time of this photograph in 1908, the whole building was owned by Littlebury's printers, who leased the front to shops.

The actual entry to The Commandery is via this door, seen here in 1951. The building is entirely wood framed, and the marks that can sometimes be seen on the timbers are keys to its assembly. The larger pieces in most timber-framed buildings would have been cut to shape on the carpenters' own premises, then assembled on site like a very large construction kit.

Above: The centre section of The Commandery's 'H' is the hall, running left to right in this photograph. Its present name comes from when the buildings were occupied by the Royalist army during the English Civil War. In August 1651, Charles II brought 18,000 troops to 'The Faithful City' (as Worcester has since been known) and billeted many of them in these buildings, with its owners, the Wylde family, who lived in the east wing. Later, The Commandery became a hospital for wounded soldiers.

Right: A closer view of the carriageway through the house. This was cut straight through the Great Hall, effectively converting it into two separate rooms. When the house passed to new owners in the twentieth century, this damage was repaired, and the Hall restored. It had not been done by 1945 though, when this photograph was taken.

Left: This is the view from the other side, taken in 1898. At this time, The Commandery was owned by Richard Mence, the vicar of Bockleton. As he was resident elsewhere, The Commandery was leased out. The closed gates over the carriageway entrance may suggest that this was no longer used.

Below: It is likely that these photographs of the interior of The Commandery date from the time when the Littlebury family were in residence. They bought the buildings in 1905 and undertook extensive restoration throughout the twentieth century; interiors were redecorated and furnished in a style sympathetic to their period. Being a printing and publishing house, the Littleburys sold postcards of their newly refurbished premises. This is the Great Hall, showing the tall leaded windows.

The garden of The Commandery looked out towards Fort Royal – another significant Civil War site. Fort Royal Hill is now a public park.

Previous page, above: The carved oak staircase, which appears to be as old as the house, displaying medieval shapes and patterns.

Previous page, below: The ornate bedroom and tester bed, like the Great Hall, look preserved but unused.

nine

Riverside

After Copenhagen Street, South Parade becomes South Quay. In this 1892 view, probably taken from the bridge, the bright weather has tempted a lot of people out for their perambulations. If this was a Sunday, the group of children at the bottom of Copenhagen Street may well be just out of the Sunday School.

Opposite, above and middle: These two panoramic views of Worcester's riverside are taken from the bridge in 1900. The top photograph shows North Parade, while the middle shows South Parade, leading to the cathedral area. The view north shows the transport of the day: apart from the pedestrians on the bridge there is river traffic parked on the east bank, a horse and cart on the far left of the west bank, and even a train steaming its way across the distant railway bridge. South of the bridge, the pleasure boats look fully laden. The cathedral, to the right, with its rural foliage, contrasts with the industrial premises further to the left.

Opposite below: A closer view of one of the river trip boats, again looking oversubscribed. It is 1912, and Worcester's famous swans are in evidence. The opening, just slightly left of centre, was Hood Street. The large building to the right (labelled Gascoine Kent – traces of the external sign-writing can still be seen on its walls) and those to the right of that have different uses today, being, respectively, an apartment building, a restaurant, and a café and restaurant. Copenhagen Street runs up alongside the café and restaurant, and two children are walking away from what is now the fountains area.

Photographed in the same year (1892) from the other side of the bridge, the Severn's sweep around the bend gives a view of both banks. On the west (right-hand) bank, a group of young men in straw boaters is inspecting the shoreline, a mother is attending to a child, and several people are lying on the grass enjoying the sun, or the view. The opposite bank has its usual complement of strollers, some with parasols.

A busy day on North Parade, looking north from the bridge in 1899. People are going about their business, carters are doing their deliveries, and even a flock of sheep is being driven along, reminding us of Worcester's rural surrounds.

Worcester has had a bridge since Roman times. The medieval bridge was replaced, in 1781, with a structure about 150m downstream, designed by John Gwynn, who died in Worcester five years later. By the mid-nineteenth century extra footpaths were added to separate pedestrians from the increasingly dangerous traffic. This photograph was taken between 1900 and 1911.

By the 1930s, the bridge was carrying so much extra traffic that the decision was made to widen it again, and plans were drawn up to build extra stonework around the original design. This rather damp ceremony is the laying of the foundation stone for the new structure. The city leaders are making their speeches while the gentlemen of the press are using the brims of their fedoras to keep the rain off their ink.

Left: When the bridge was widened, the old toll houses were demolished. It is not known when the bridge stopped charging for crossings, but this toll house, on the west side of the river, had been disused for many years. The tower in the background belongs to All Saints' church, at the junction of Quay Street and Bridge Street.

Below: In this 1932 photograph, the bridge is clearly much wider, and before its official opening (that October), is closed to traffic, making it seem even more spacious. All Saints' is right of centre, the riverside industrial area is in full smoke, and enormous bridge-side posters implore people to contribute to the fund for extending the infirmary and through-travellers to stop and shop in Worcester's Shopping Week, timed for just after the opening of the bridge.

Above: Among the risks of a riverside city is that of flooding, and Worcester has known many floods. The flood of 1947 was one of the worst, and nearly filled the bridge's arches. The river continued to rise after this photograph was taken.

Below: Floods have been recorded in Worcester since 1484, though the Water Gate's records only remember as far back as 1672. The January 1899 flood shown here, although severe in itself, was thirteen years after one of the worst in the Water Gate's historical record. 250 houses were affected, and a pike was caught in the sitting room of The Old Rectifying House (the timber building with four gables).

Since the bridge was widened in 1932, the space in front of The Old Rectifying House has become a much busier road. This view from the other side of the inn shows how the water level in 1947 had risen over that of the nineteenth-century floods. It is now right up to the ground-floor windowsills.

The Old Rectifying House's name comes from the rectification, or repeated distillation, of spirits. A distillery used to be part of the building. It is accustomed to flooding, and beer casks are repeatedly rescued from the cellars and taken upstairs. Deliveries, and sometimes customers, had to make their entry through the upstairs windows. It is fortunate, therefore, that the building was designed with a galleried front. Potential customers are here considering the likelihood of negotiating the precarious arrangement of plank and ladder to get into the bar, and maybe the even more precarious exit later.

The 1947 flood seen in this view makes Worcester seem like a lakeside city. The water has flowed across the riverbanks and up Copenhagen Street.

Looking like it is in danger of becoming engulfed, the cathedral stands like Mont St Michel over a watery world. The year of this particular flood is not recorded.

Looking as if they are marooned on an island, this family contemplate their escape up Copenhagen Street. The arches are now almost completely filled with water in this 1947 photograph.

Resembling a snow scene, this is the 1947 flood further upstream, turning Pitchcroft racecourse and its surrounds into a lake.

ten

The Shambles
to Cornmarket

There are two memorable buildings in these photographs: St Swithin's church, and the black and white premises of J. and F. Hall, seen before in the Church Street photographs. This view is from the early 1960s and shows a busy shopping day, possibly a Saturday.

This more aerial view is from 1935 and is almost as busy as the one above. The Shambles is a traditional name for butchers, who originally sold their wares in markets. Worcester's Shambles has always been a busy shopping street, though its relatively narrow width, combined with traffic, perhaps made it seem busier before it was pedestrianised.

Twelve noon (if H. Samuel's clock is accurate) on a day in June 1964. As we know, J. and F. Hall's premises did not survive very long into the thoroughly modern '60s, but life in the Shambles is as busy as ever.

A quiet Shambles, perhaps due to the rain. This is an early 1960s shot, with Hall's building in the distance, jutting out into the street. The shops of St Swithin's Street can be seen at the end.

Above: A view in the same direction, but taken from further back at the Pump Street junction, sometime in the mid–1960s, and looking down the whole length of a very busy Shambles.

Below, left: In 1961, Hall's occupied the building next door, too. It is here advertising a 'Bargain Sale'.

Below, right: The scene could be Covent Garden, but in fact it's a flower market outside the front of St Swithin's church, and these ladies are looking for some bargain spring daffodils.

Above: Perhaps in this street of butchers, A.F. Eden felt the need to outdo – this exotic display must have tempted many people. Not only did the appropriately named Mr Eden have all these heavenly delights, but he was aware of the use of technology to speed up the sales process.

Right: Trinity Street is the northerly continuation of The Shambles, and its key feature is Queen Elizabeth's House. The Queen visited Worcester in 1575, and legend has it that she addressed the crowds from the gallery. The more likely root of the name, however, is through an endowment to the Trinity Hospital, of which it was a part. The most interesting part of its history, though, is its avoidance of demolition in 1891. Street remodelling was in progress then, too, and the house was in the way. Protestors formed a restoration committee, and managed to raise enough money to physically move the house, on screw jacks and rails, a distance of 30ft. It was said to have weighed over 200 tons. The photograph dates from March 1907, and the boys may well be going to the school at the end of the road, next to St Martin's church.

The Trinity runs at a right angle to Trinity Street, from Queen Elizabeth's House to what is now the Cornmarket. It also runs in the other direction, up to The Cross, and this is the section that has the bridge on it. This is what it looked like in the 1890s, as a young apprentice poses in front of the old Bridge House and Trinity Hall. The view is from The Cross end, with St Martin's church tower in the distance.

In 1915 Worcester was still in touch with its rural roots, as the town centre still had this old tythe barn in The Trinity. St Martin's church tower looms large.

Trinity Hall is at the end of its days, and surviving as an advertising board. The top of
St Nicholas' church can be seen over its roof line.

Queen Street runs parallel to Trinity Street, and this is a view from its St Nicholas Street end.
The building on the right is the old Worcester Co-operative building, since replaced with a much
less interesting-looking store. All the buildings on the left are gone, and the view is now directly
into Cornmarket's car park. The most distant building is Cornmarket's Public Hall which is in the
process of demolition in July 1966.

Looking east from the Cornmarket in the direction of this (possibly Edwardian) photograph, you will now see the City Walls Road, a roundabout, and H.A. Fox's Jaguar dealership. Then, St Martin's Gate (leading to St Martin's church, behind the photographer and slightly to his left) was the road to the right, between the shops in the middle distance and the Plough Inn, which can be seen on the far left. Turning right, in front of L.F. Batten, you would be facing King Charles' House and the entrance to New Street.

Opposite above: This is how the Public Hall looked from the front early in 1966. It was a concert hall used for, among other things, the Three Choirs Festival during Worcester's turn to host.

Opposite below: The Cornmarket is the space between the Public Hall, Mealcheapen Street and New Street. Nowadays, it refers to the whole area, including the car park that has replaced the Public Hall and the area behind it. Mealcheapen Street runs into the distance in this photograph, taken in February 1966, after the Royal Exchange inn (now the Exchange).

This is King Charles' House in Cornmarket, in 1951. The entrance to New Street is to the right past the seed shop. During the Civil War, King Charles escaped the Parliamentarian forces from this house and left the city via St Martin's Gate, the only exit not covered by Cromwell's men. Confusingly, a similar house exists around the corner in New Street, and there has been debate about which is really King Charles' House.

The answer, of course, is that they are both the same house, as this illustration from 1799 clearly shows. This imposing house suffered fire damage that destroyed the upper floor and the entire corner, and effectively split it in two. The house (or houses) had the roofline lowered, but the corner was demolished and an infill building, in the modern style, added.

The Plough Inn in Silver Street, opposite the Cornmarket, with a white-hatted couple on the right about to walk down St Martin's Gate, 1914. The inn is responding to changing times by offering both stabling and garaging. It retained its Georgian lines for many years.

The Plough was the first building on Silver Street, which all but disappeared at the end of the 1960s as part of the new traffic system. Prior to that, at sometime during its history, the Plough had lost its next-door neighbour and had been remodelled in the Tudor style. How much of this was restoration, or how much cosmetic attachment is not clear.

Above: Exchange Street has completely disappeared since this 1970 photograph. It ran down what is now the centre of Cornmarket car park, from east to west, a continuation of The Trinity. The Public Hall backed on to it, and probably gave it its most use, along with J. and F. Hall, who had warehousing there.

Left: This fine old black pear tree, something of a symbol for Worcester, was in the grounds of the Public Hall, next to Silver Street. It was cut down in 1955.

eleven

Routes Through

Left: Lowesmoor is the road that leads north-east from Cornmarket, though these days a dual carriageway needs to be crossed to get there. It has been an area of industry and poverty, much like the riverside section of the city. This house, photographed in March 1922, could well have been at the front of a court of other dwellings, and was being used to sell fish and chips.

Below: It is not known when this photograph was taken, but it portrays the last thatched house in Worcester city. It was located $\frac{9}{10}$ of a mile from The Cross, in Rainbow Hill.

Above: Lowesmoor continues away from the city centre and divides into Lowesmoor Terrace and Lowesmoor Place, the former leading into Rainbow Hill and the latter leading to this view, with another fork; the left goes to what is now Tolladine Road, but at the time of this photograph led only to the gas works, and the other, to the right, is Shrub Hill Road, leading to the railway station. Dominating the junction is the Heenan and Froude factory, an impressive Victorian Italianate landmark.

Below: Heenan and Froude factory, seen from Shrub Hill Road in the 1950s. Its clock is clearly visible even at this end, and its cream and red brickwork give it a unique look.

It was not always the factory of Heenan and Froude. It started life as the engineering works for the railway station, and changed hands several times. It was, fortunately, empty at the time of the Worcester Exhibition, and proved an ideal location for it. The official opening is recorded here, and at the centre of the photograph is a carriage carrying an unnamed VIP. The crowd seems to consist of a great number of policemen.

Opposite above: Holy Trinity church was next door to the Heenan and Froude factory in Shrub Hill Road. Its distinguishing feature was its beamed roof, which had been rescued from the Guesten Hall of Worcester Cathedral when it was demolished. Then, in turn, Holy Trinity church was demolished in the late 1960s and the roof was taken to the Avoncroft Museum of Historic Buildings, where it can, by virtue of being on a lower building, be appreciated more widely. The vicar, Revd Nankivell, is here watching the choir boys removing paint from the railings, though the use of hammers to do this seems more like a penance than an efficient use of their time.

Opposite below: The Old Palace, or Deanery, is hidden away behind a wall in Deansway, a road designed to carry traffic out of the city as rapidly as possible. It used to be the residence of the bishop until Hartlebury Castle was chosen to replace it.

Merry Vale has been swallowed up in the Deansway development, but was the road that Quay Street became before curving around All Saints' church. This 1905 photograph shows a housing community typical of the busy but overcrowded area east of the river.

This building, Northwall House, fortunately survives, though it is quite sheltered in The Butts, and its gardens have been replaced by industrial units. It recently went through a period of dereliction, but was saved. Although it is private accommodation now, at the time of this photograph it was part of Worcester Grammar School for Girls.

Opposite: Albert Simons had this shop at the corner of Sansome Walk and Wood Terrace. Here he poses happily with his family, cat and a well-turned-out shop display.

New Street leads to Friar Street, whose impressive stock of timber-framed architecture remains unchanged for most of its length (the exceptions being at the Sidbury end). In New Street, a few doors away from King Charles' House, the Pheasant Inn shows its heritage (in this 1908 photograph), offering wines, spirits and good stabling.

Further Along New Street, towards Friar Street, Nash's House stands out as a fine example of the wood-builder's craft. In 1905 it housed a picture-frame manufacturer. Looking at this photograph, the popularity of galoshes can be understood. Much trailing of the mud must have happened in an afternoon's shopping.

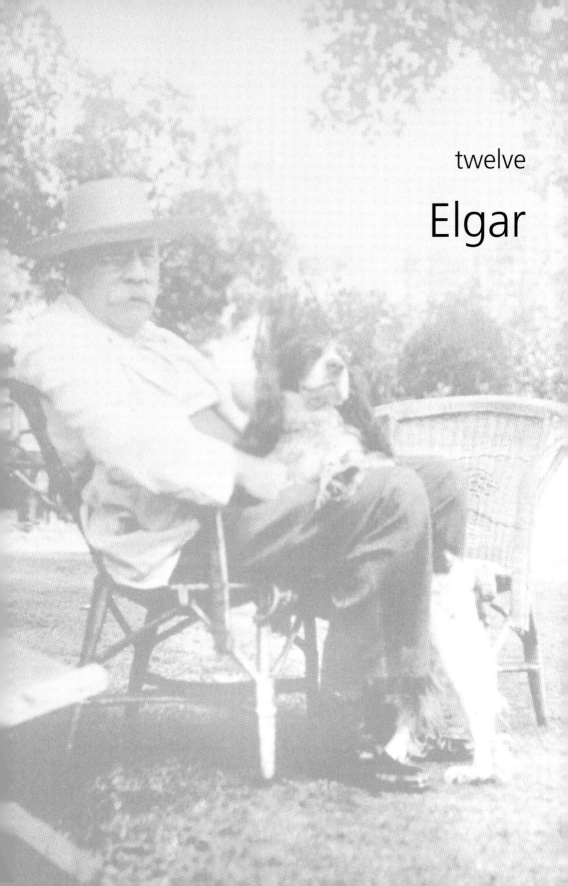

twelve

Elgar

Sir Edward Elgar was a man of Worcester, in the sense that not only did he live here, but he was an enthusiast for the area. The landscape inspired him, and his love for music was developed at home as a boy, and in his father's shop in the High Street. After some time in London, he returned to Worcester in 1929 to this house, Marl Bank, on Rainbow Hill. It was to be his last home. (Copyright The Elgar Birthplace Museum)

Elgar posed for this photograph while composing in his studio at Marl Bank, in 1932. In this year Worcester's bridge was being widened. Elgar was so fond of the iron balustrades that were being replaced that he bought some sections and had them installed in his garden. (Copyright The Elgar Birthplace Museum)

Elgar enjoyed the company of his dogs, Marco and Mina, and following the death of his wife involved himself with them more regularly. Marl Bank had a good, dog-friendly garden, and the house was also the location of some of Elgar's late work. He had a radio link installed to the HMV London recording studios in order to be able to comment on the method and quality of the recording of his work. (Copyright The Elgar Birthplace Museum)

Elgar entertained in his Rainbow Hill garden. Along with Elgar's dog, Marco, are friends Barry Jackson, creator of the Malvern Festival, and Scott Sunderland. (Copyright The Elgar Birthplace Museum)

SIR EDWARD ELGAR
LIVED IN THIS HOUSE
FROM 1929 TO 1934

After his death in 1934, Marl Bank bore this plaque to commemorate Elgar's presence there. The house, however, has not survived, and not even the plaque remains to tell passers-by that Elgar once lived here. The land has been used to build low-rise flats, now known as Elgar Court.

The Freedom of the City came to Sir Edward in 1905. He is seen here leaving the Guildhall after receiving the award, accompanied by the Lord Mayor. (Copyright The Elgar Birthplace Museum)

The first recording of Elgar's cello concerto, now closely associated with the cellist Jacqueline du Pré, was made in 1919 with Beatrice Harrison, seen here with the composer in the studio. (Copyright The Elgar Birthplace Museum)

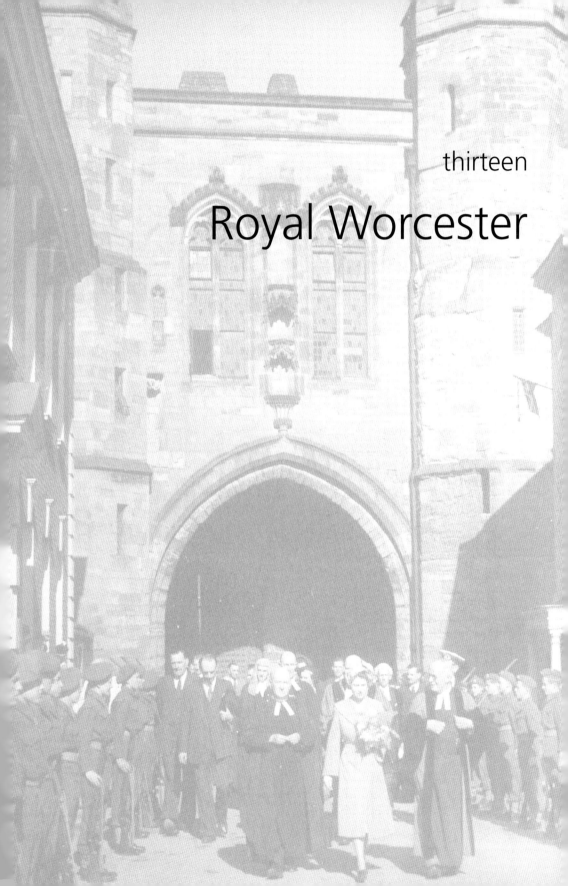

thirteen

Royal Worcester

Worcester has received many royal visits over the years: King John and Prince Arthur are buried in the cathedral; Queen Elizabeth I visited in 1575 and, perhaps the most significant of all for the city, Charles II fought a battle here before escaping the city and Parliamentarian forces. The only royal visitors to be photographed, of course, have been from the twentieth century. Neither the date nor the event are recorded for this photograph, but it depicts the occasion of a visit to The Cross by the Duke of York, the future King George V, who held the title from 1892 and became King in 1910. The next Duke of York title was not conferred until 1920, when it became the designation of Prince Albert (the future King George VI).

Above: When Worcester's bridge was widened for traffic, the Prince of Wales visited for its official inauguration in 1932. An enormous crowd, backing up to Bridge Street and beyond, turned out for the occasion. Prince Edward was later to find fame – or notoriety – as the king who abdicated in 1936. (Copyright *Sunday Mercury*)

Right: Princess Elizabeth visited Worcester on 8 June 1951. Crowds flocked to the city centre to see her at various points of the tour. Naturally, she explored the cathedral and its surrounds and is seen here below the Edgar Tower. (Copyright *Sunday Mercury*)

A cavalcade of extremely shiny cars took Princess Elizabeth to The Guildhall where a civic
reception awaited. The High Street had two-way traffic in those days, and the old market hall
is still there.

Making her greetings or farewells, the future queen is suitably framed by the Guildhall's wrought
ironwork.

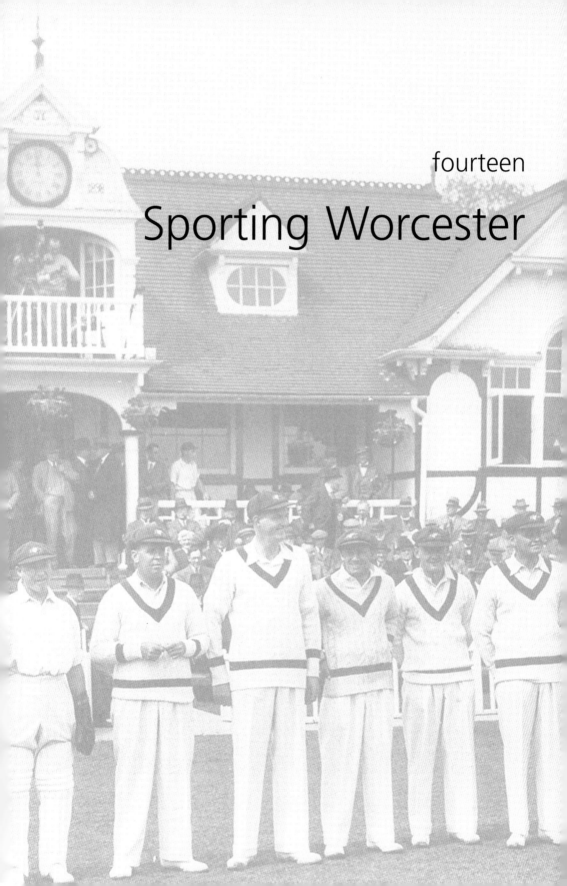

fourteen

Sporting Worcester

Above: Worcester has two wonderful advantages over most cities: it has a very good racecourse at Pitchcroft and a beautiful and famous cricket ground in New Road. This bustling scene at Pitchcroft on a race day dates from the late 1960s or early '70s, before the grandstand was built.

Below: The grandstand in progress during the 1970s.

Above: Sir Desmond Plummer unveils the plaque to signify the official opening of the new grandstand on 23 April 1975; St George's day and also Shakespeare's birthday.

Right: Looking south, in the direction of the river's flow, it can be seen just how vulnerable the racecourse is to flooding. The river flows nearby, and its course can be followed until just after the railway bridge. An attractive view of the earth from the air, but unpleasant for those on the ground.

Worcestershire Cricket Club is a venerable society with a well-respected tradition. This is the team from the first club match in 1899, not long after its formation. Members are, from left to right, back row: ? Wheldon, ? Wilson, Paul Foley, ? Arnold, ? Burrows. Middle row: W.L. Foster, E. Bromley-Martin, H.K. Foster, R.E. Foster, G. Bromley-Martin. Front: ? Straw, A. Bird. (Copyright Worcestershire County Cricket Club)

Opposite above: The 1934 Australian team photographed in front of the pavilion. They were about to play Worcestershire, and the match was to be filmed from the balcony. (Copyright Worcestershire County Cricket Club)

Opposite below: The Australian tourists of 1938, led by Don Bradman (seated), visiting the Royal Porcelain Works. (Copyright Worcestershire County Cricket Club)

Another royal visit, this time from Queen Elizabeth II in April 1957. The Queen and Prince Philip were driven around the cricket ground by The Queen's Own Worcestershire Yeomanry. (Copyright Worcestershire County Cricket Club)

Dr W.G. Grace, that legend of cricket, then aged fifty-one, leaving after scoring 175 for the London County XI. Dr Grace was a frequent visitor to New Road, playing as he did for Gloucestershire until a late move to London. (Copyright Worcestershire County Cricket Club)

Other local titles published by Tempus

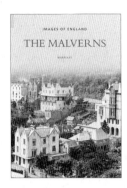

The Malverns
BRIAN ILES

This collection of over 200 archive photographs documents life in the Malverns from the 1860s until the 1950s. All aspects of everyday life are featured here, including shops and businesses, work and leisure and the war years. Local events such as the Bicycle Carnivals at Malvern Link are also recalled. *The Malverns* will delight those who want to know more about the history of the area.

0 7524 3667 8

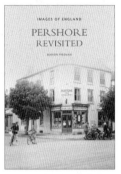

Pershore Revisited
MARION FREEMAN

This collection of over 200 archive photographs reveals some of the changes that have taken place in the Worcestershire town of Pershore over the last century. The Pershore Festival, Empire Day celebrations and the annual fair, fruit harvests and hop-picking are some of the local events featured here. This volume explores all aspects of everyday life, from shops and businesses to churches and schools.

0 7524 3737 2

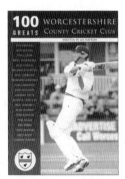

Worcestershire County Cricket Club 100 Greats
LES HATTON

Worcestershire celebrated 100 years of first-class cricket in 1999. The seven Foster brothers were members of the side in the early days, three of them appearing in the first Championship match at New Road against Yorkshire, but times were so hard after the First World War that the county did not enter the competition in 1919. Among\ these great Worcestershire cricketers are Ted Arnold, Albert Bird, Fred Bowley, Dick Burrows and George Wilson, all members of the team during that first 1899 season.

0 7524 2194 8

Herefordshire Life: Photographs by Derek Evans
KEITH JAMES

This volume illustrates some of the many people and places photographed by Derek Evans over the past fifty years or more and is a fitting tribute to the county. From images of cider-apple factories and the chairman of Hereford United Football Club, Len Weston, to visiting hop-picking families and the Friendly Society's annual club walk, this book will appeal to all those who know the area as it is and provide a welcome glimpse into Herefordshire past and its people for others.

0 7524 3724 0

If you are interested in purchasing other books published by Tempus, or in case you have difficulty finding any Tempus books in your local bookshop, you can also place orders directly through our website

www.tempus-publishing.com